Let's Go to the Store!

grocery store

bananas
bread
sandwich
cake

store

Casual
Casual
Casual
Jacken
big labels small prices
$19,99
$14,99
$24,99

$19.99

shoes
socks
shorts
shoes

book store

BARGAIN BOOKS
new books added daily

crayons
Max
Goes Shopping
by Adria F. Klein
illustrated by
Mernie Gallagher-Cole
NATIONAL GEOGRAPHIC
Windows on Literacy™
Shopping with Dad
Lesley Pether
books